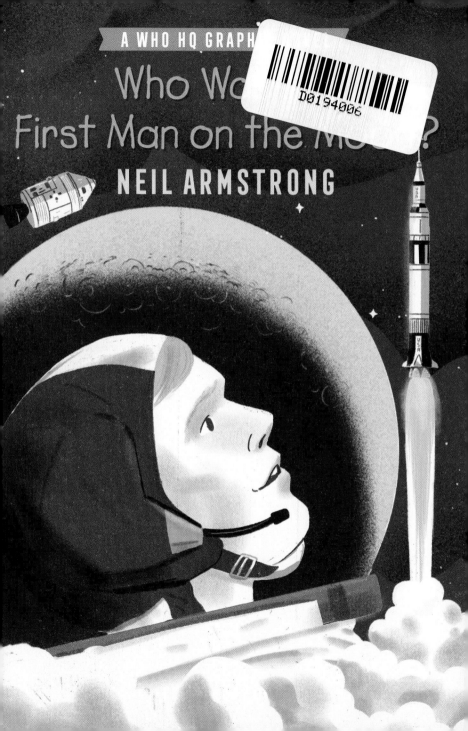

Who Wo
First Man on the Mo
NEIL ARMSTRONG

For Cameron and Hayden—NP

In loving memory of Shirley Dennis.
Thank you, Grandma—DS

No part of this publication may be reproduced, stored in a retrieval system, or transmitted in any form or by any means, electronic, mechanical, photocopying, recording, or otherwise, without written permission of the publisher. For information regarding permission, write to Penguin Workshop, Permissions Department, 1745 Broadway, 15th Floor, New York, NY 10019.

ISBN 978-1-338-87112-8

12 11 10 9 8 7 6 5 4 3 2   22 23 24 25 26 27

Printed in the U.S.A.   40

First Scholastic printing, September 2022

Image on TV on page 56 courtesy NASA

Lettering by Comicraft

Book design by Jay Emmanuel

A WHO HQ GRAPHIC NOVEL

Who Was the First Man on the Moon?

NEIL ARMSTRONG

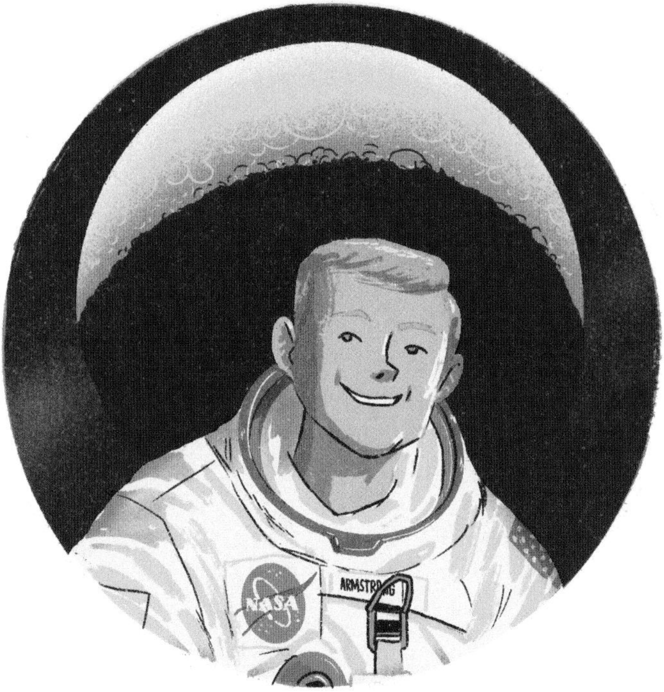

NASA
ARMSTRONG

by Nathan Page

illustrated by Drew Shannon

SCHOLASTIC INC.

Introduction

Neil Armstrong was born August 5, 1930, on the edge of a small farming town called Wapakoneta, Ohio, where the land is flat and on a clear day the skies are limitless.

Neil loved reading, building model planes, and looking after his younger siblings. He experimented a lot as a boy, tinkering, exploring, and always wanting to learn more about the world around him. Sometimes Neil's experiments were outright disasters. But with each disaster, he became more familiar with risk and when it was a good time to take one.

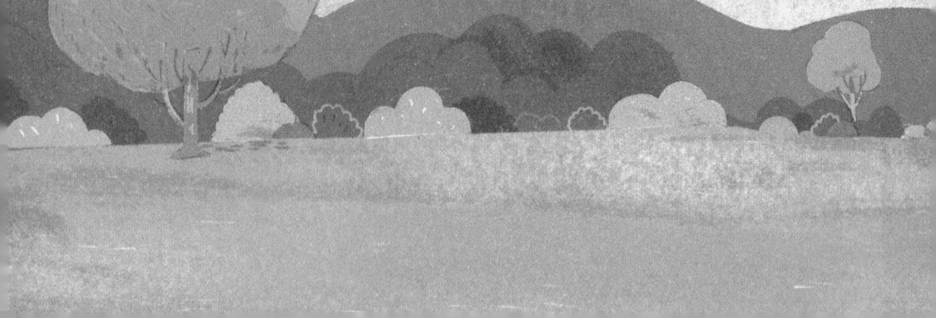

His curiosity with the world continued throughout his life. He learned how to fly planes when he was still in high school, served as a Navy pilot during the Korean War, and then graduated from college as an aeronautical engineer. He was a pilot of experimental planes like the X-15, and because of his reputation for being able to fly any aircraft, in 1962, NASA selected him to be among their second group of astronauts.

On July 16, 1969, Neil set out on a spaceflight with his fellow crew members, Buzz Aldrin and Michael Collins, at the Kennedy Space Center in Cape Canaveral, Florida. All systems were go: The crew at the NASA Mission Control Center located in Houston, Texas, was ready for liftoff, and the entire world was watching. Neil had no idea how this experiment would unfold—all he knew was that he wasn't in Wapakoneta anymore. And this time, there was no room for mistakes.

Every experiment, every takeoff and landing, all the falls and moments too close to call, got Neil to July 20, 1969: the day he became the first man to walk on the moon.

This was known as the Apollo 11 mission.

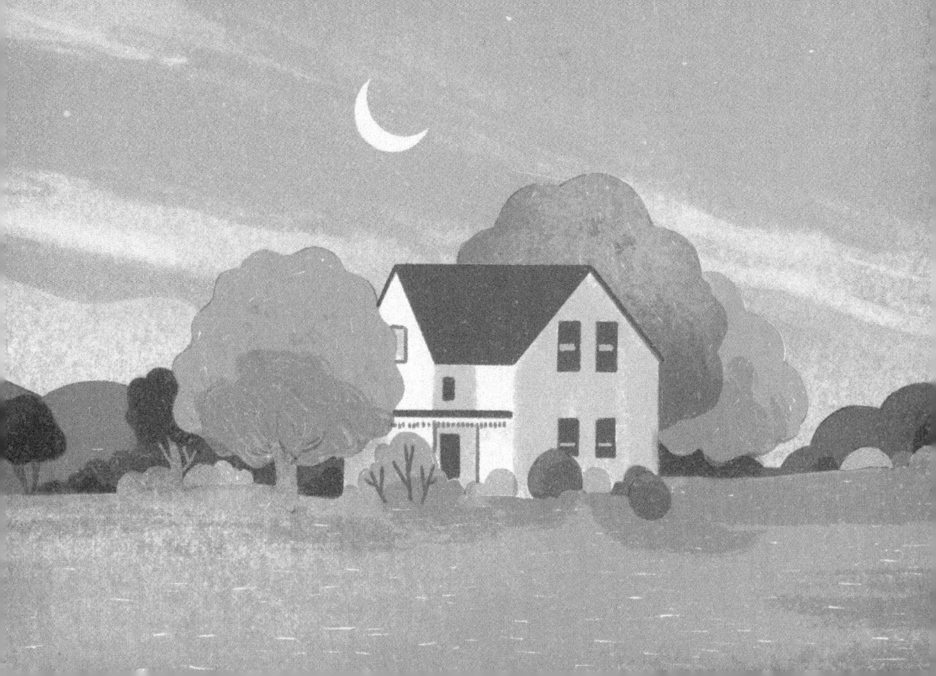

6

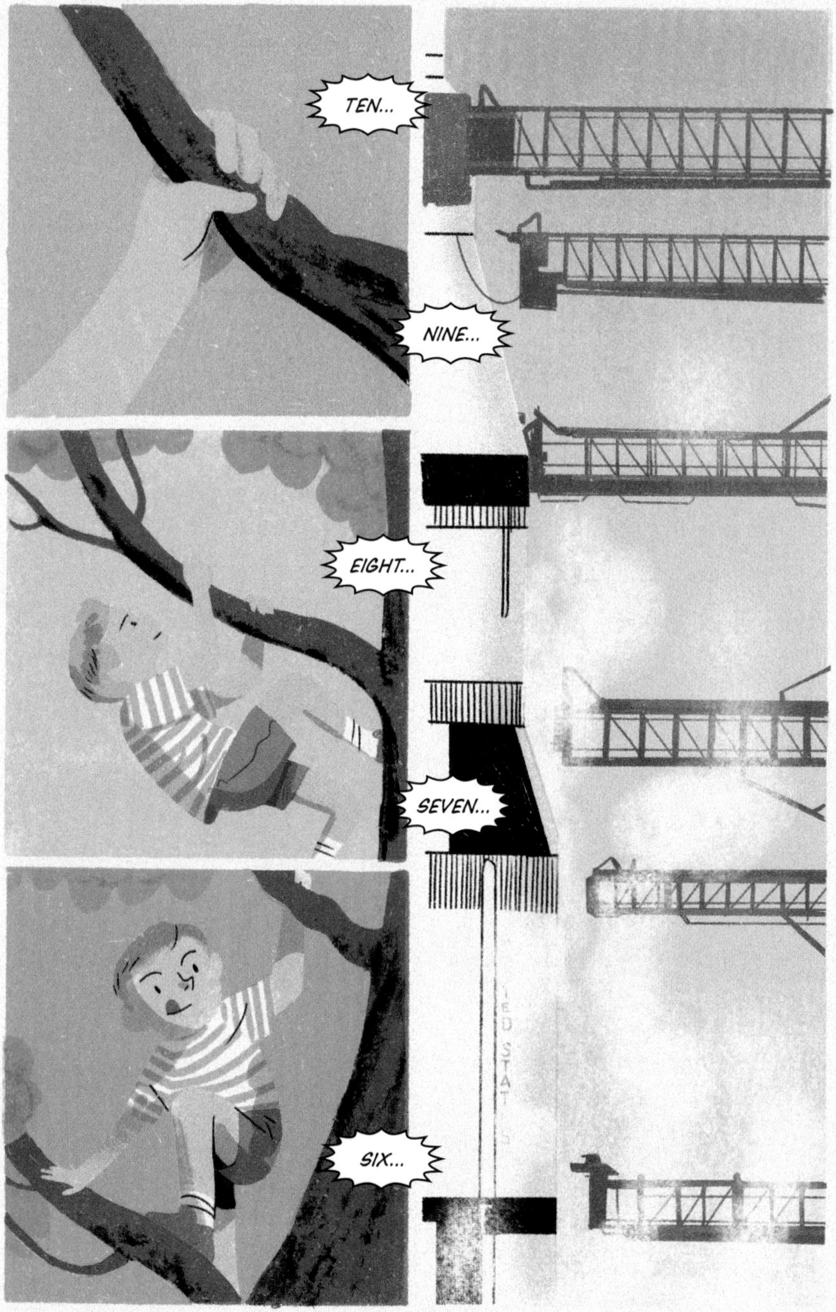
TEN...
NINE...
EIGHT...
SEVEN...
SIX...

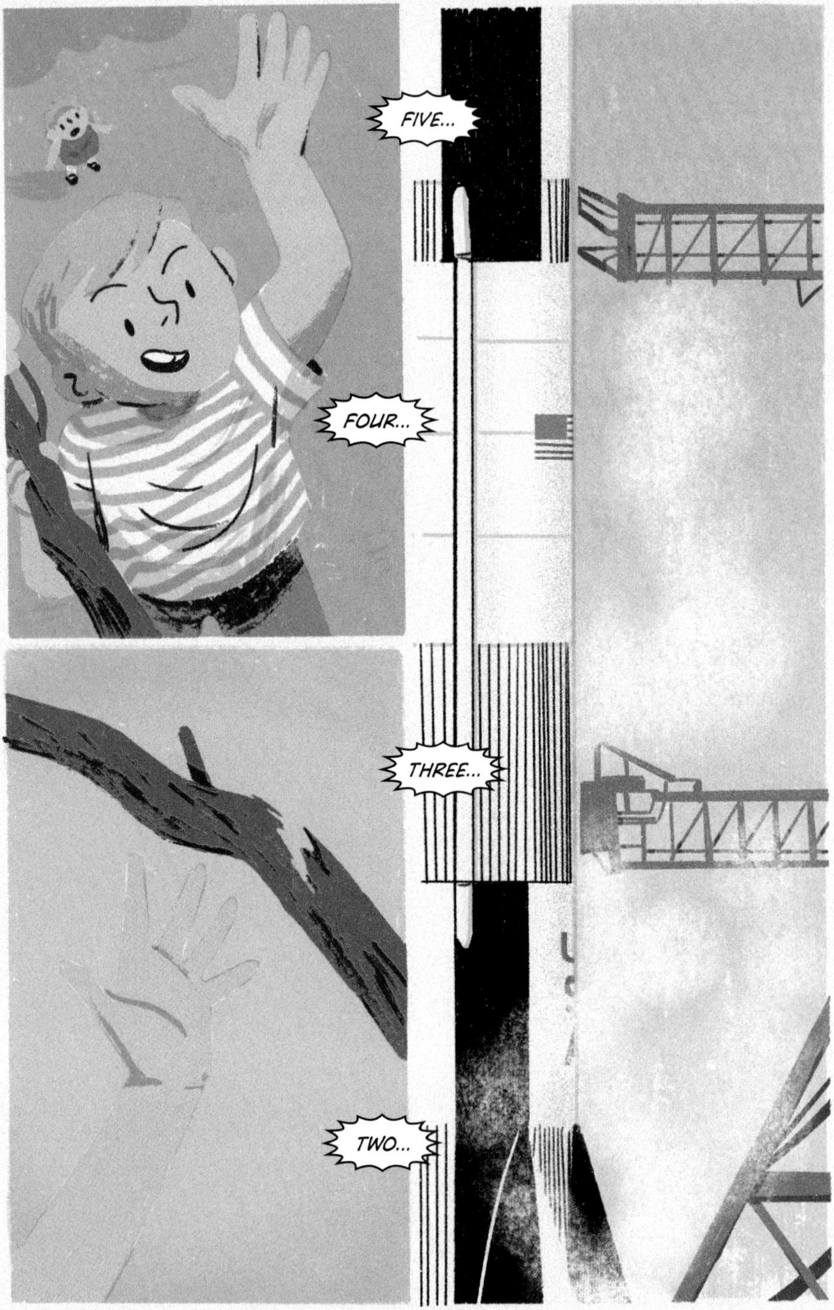
FIVE...
FOUR...
THREE...
TWO...

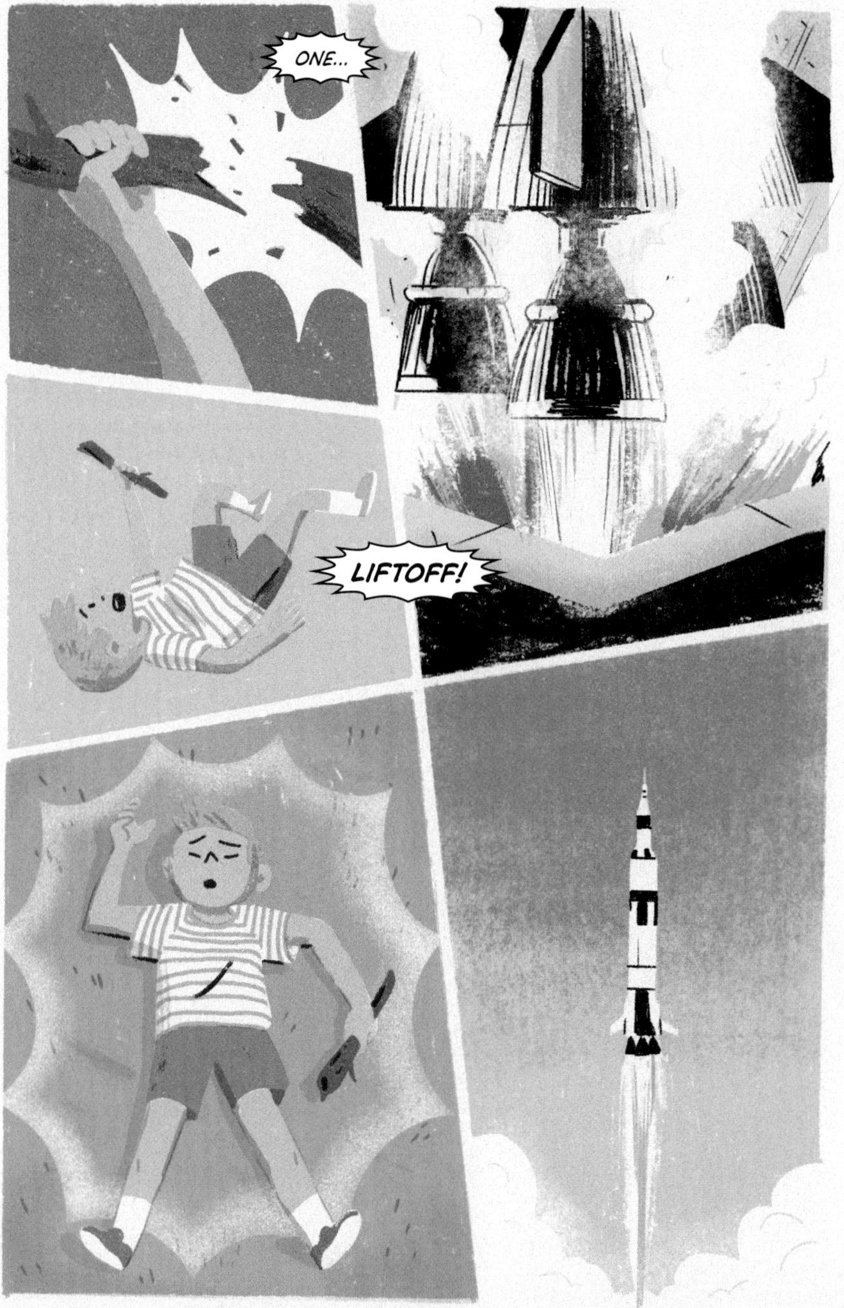
ONE...
LIFTOFF!

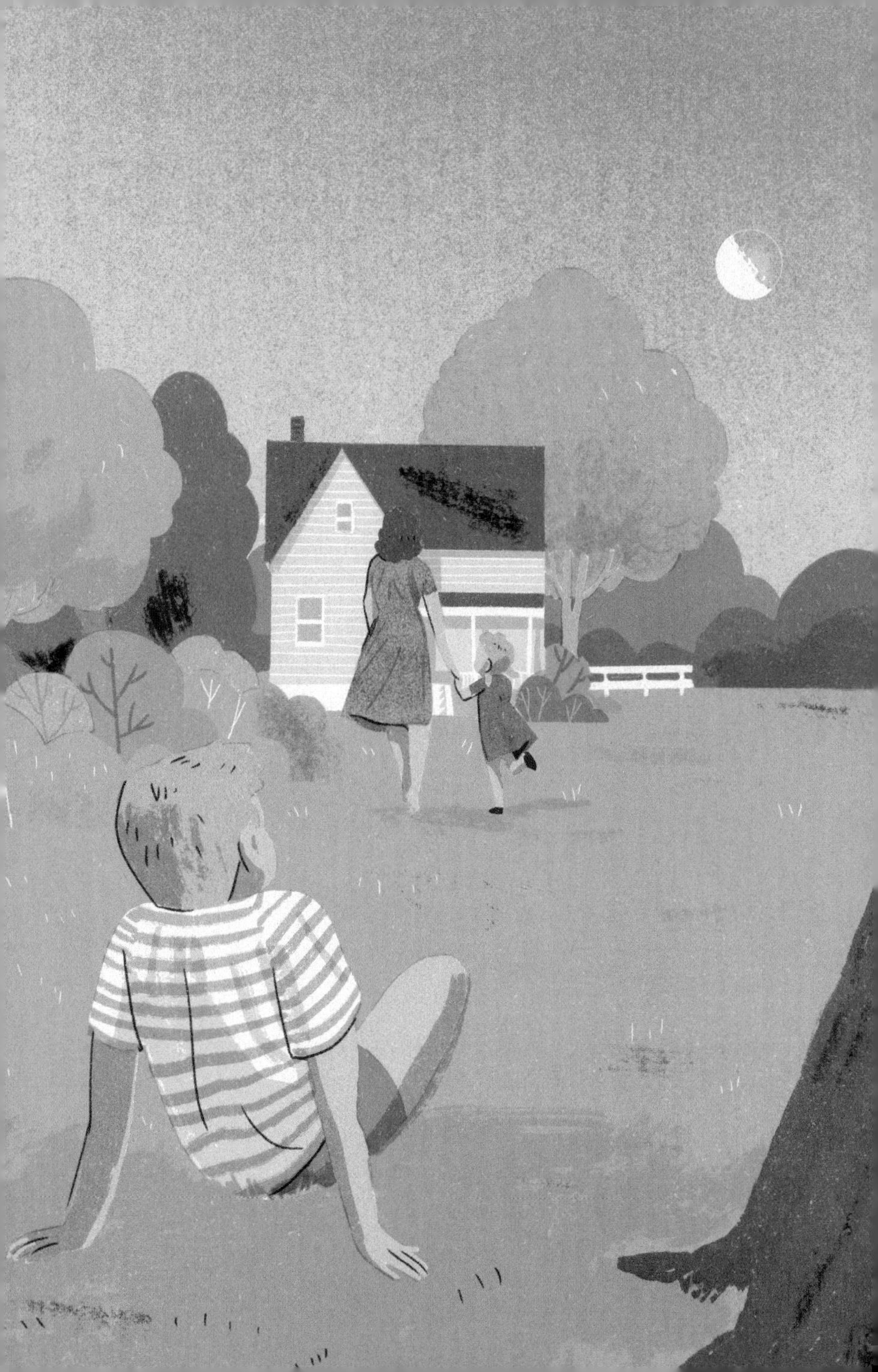

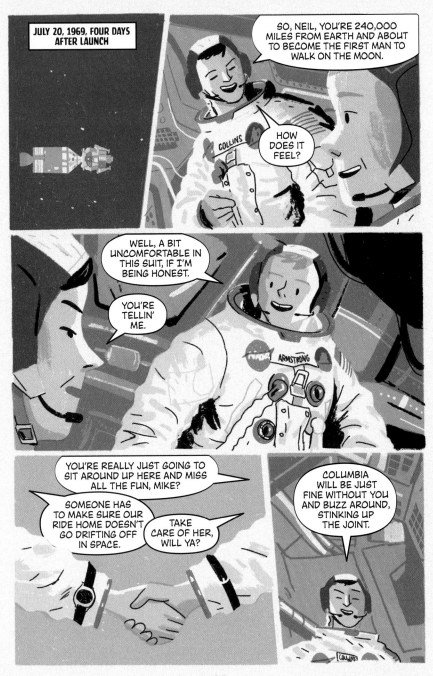

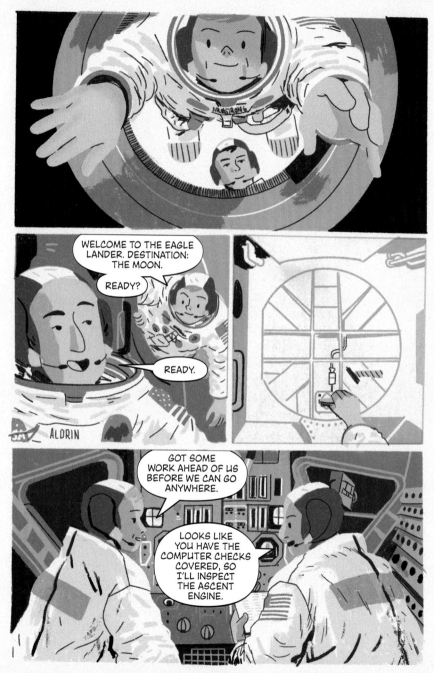

13

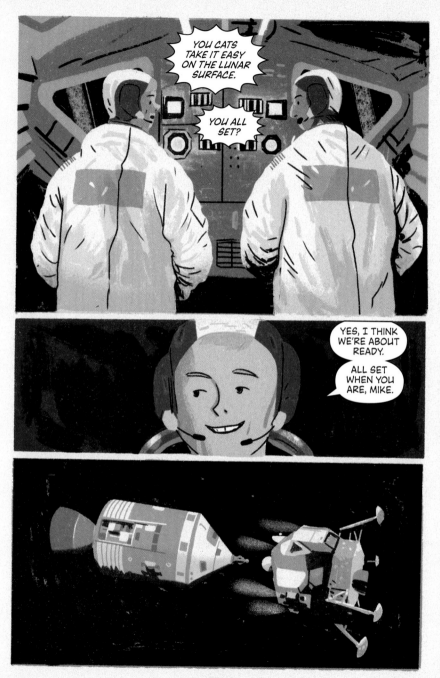

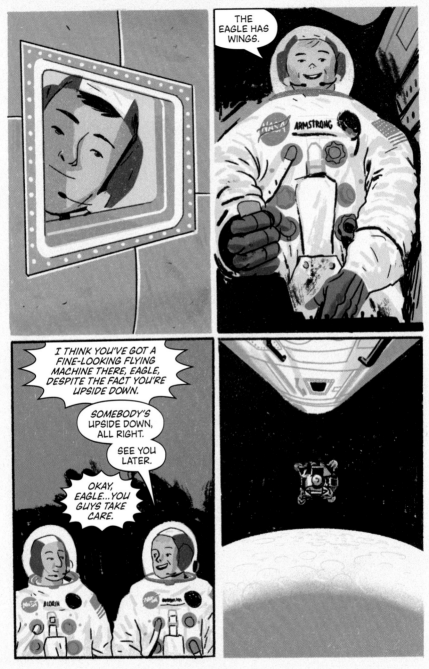

16

Michael Collins

Michael Collins was born on October 31, 1930, in Rome, Italy, where his father, Major General James Collins, was stationed in the military. Curious and very clever, Michael loved to read and enjoyed building model planes. He played on his high-school football team and went on to attend the United States Military Academy at West Point, where he graduated with a bachelor of science in 1952.

Michael served as a fighter pilot as well as an experimental test pilot prior to being selected to join the third group of NASA astronauts in 1963. With NASA, he was the pilot of Gemini 10, a mission in which he became just the third American ever to complete an EVA (extravehicular activity). Or, to put it in simpler and cooler terms, he spacewalked!

For the Apollo 11 mission, Michael became the pilot of Columbia, the command module that stayed behind while Neil and Buzz completed their journey to the moon. After the mission, Michael received the 1969 Presidential Medal of Freedom and was also awarded the 2011 Congressional Gold Medal, two of the highest awards a civilian can receive in the United States.

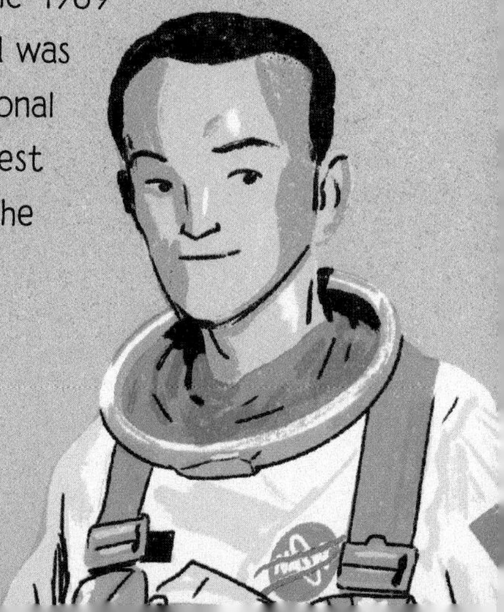

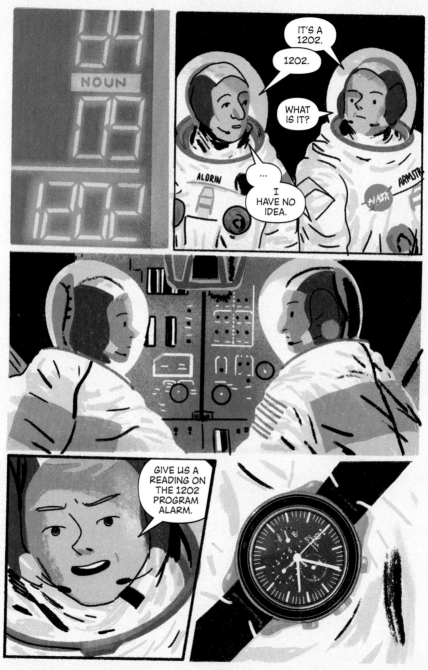

19

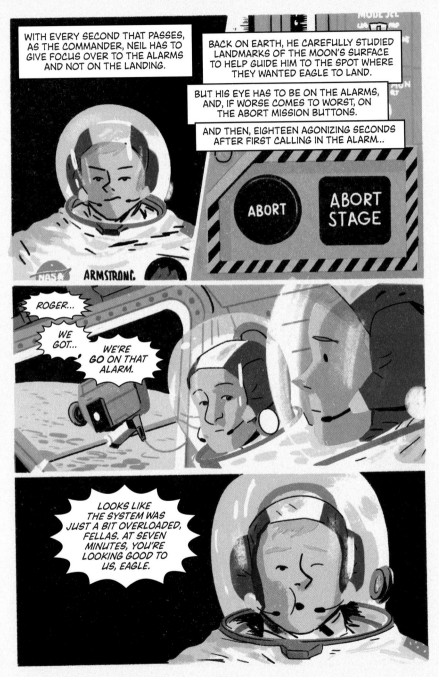

WITH EVERY SECOND THAT PASSES, AS THE COMMANDER, NEIL HAS TO GIVE FOCUS OVER TO THE ALARMS AND NOT ON THE LANDING.

BACK ON EARTH, HE CAREFULLY STUDIED LANDMARKS OF THE MOON'S SURFACE TO HELP GUIDE HIM TO THE SPOT WHERE THEY WANTED EAGLE TO LAND.

BUT HIS EYE HAS TO BE ON THE ALARMS, AND, IF WORSE COMES TO WORST, ON THE ABORT MISSION BUTTONS.

AND THEN, EIGHTEEN AGONIZING SECONDS AFTER FIRST CALLING IN THE ALARM...

ABORT

ABORT STAGE

NASA ARMSTRONG

ROGER...

WE GOT...

WE'RE GO ON THAT ALARM.

LOOKS LIKE THE SYSTEM WAS JUST A BIT OVERLOADED, FELLAS. AT SEVEN MINUTES, YOU'RE LOOKING GOOD TO US, EAGLE.

Eagle, the Apollo 11 Lunar Module

Designed for the sole purpose of landing on and taking off from the moon, the lunar module (known as Eagle for the Apollo 11 mission) was actually two different spacecrafts put together: one to land on the moon and the other to rejoin Columbia and go back home.

Inside, there were no seats for the astronauts because the craft had to be light enough to fly. In fact, Neil and Buzz were standing for the whole flight. Another way NASA engineers reduced weight was by cutting down the size of the windows. So by the time that Neil and Buzz were standing at the controls, there was not much space for the astronauts to even look outside.

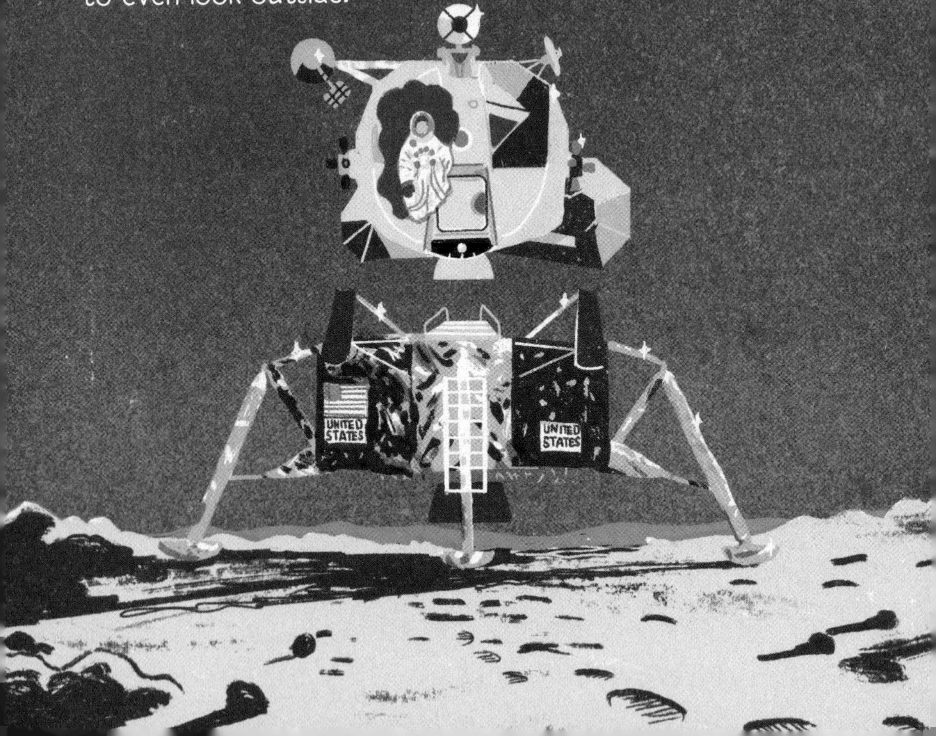

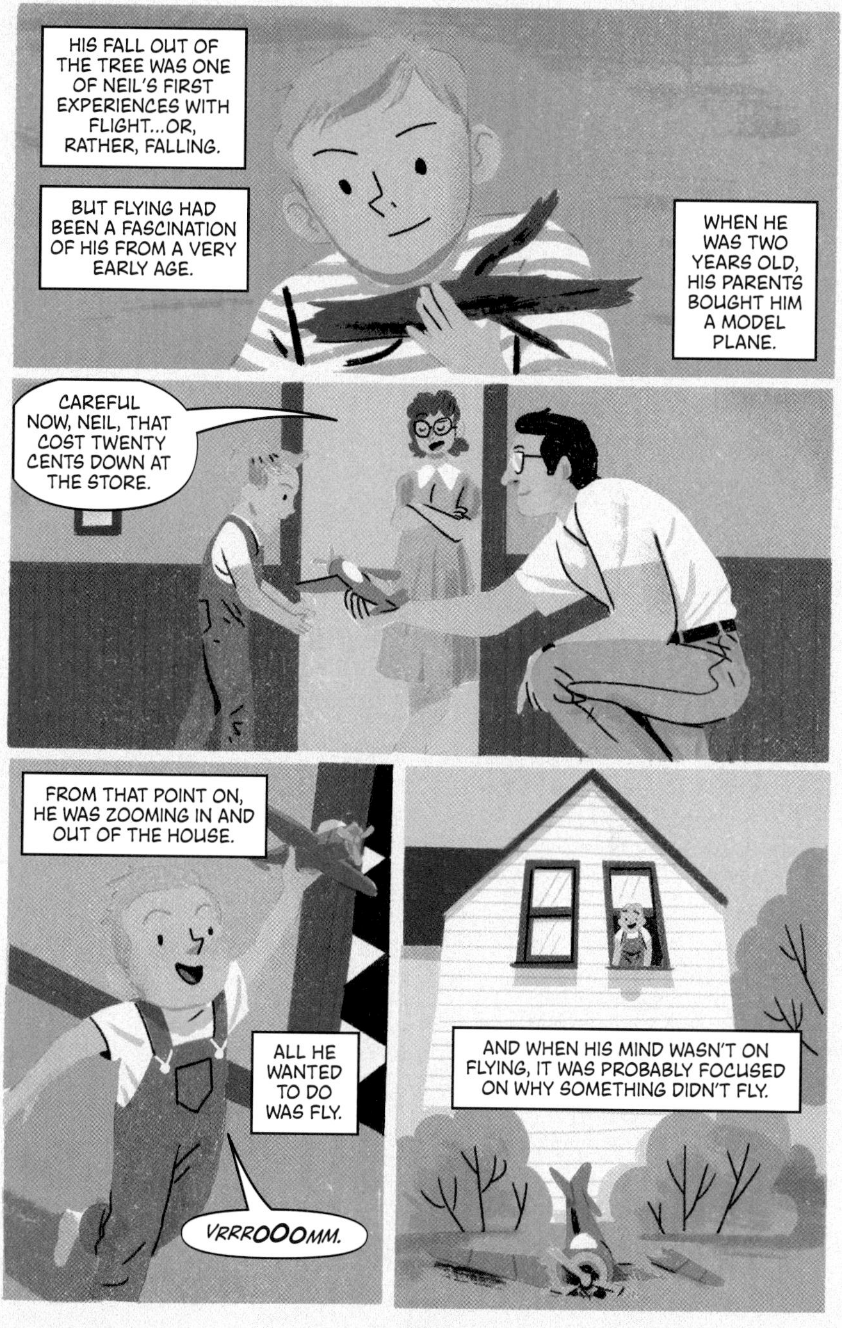
HIS FALL OUT OF THE TREE WAS ONE OF NEIL'S FIRST EXPERIENCES WITH FLIGHT...OR, RATHER, FALLING.
BUT FLYING HAD BEEN A FASCINATION OF HIS FROM A VERY EARLY AGE.
WHEN HE WAS TWO YEARS OLD, HIS PARENTS BOUGHT HIM A MODEL PLANE.
CAREFUL NOW, NEIL, THAT COST TWENTY CENTS DOWN AT THE STORE.
FROM THAT POINT ON, HE WAS ZOOMING IN AND OUT OF THE HOUSE.
ALL HE WANTED TO DO WAS FLY.
VRRROOOMM.
AND WHEN HIS MIND WASN'T ON FLYING, IT WAS PROBABLY FOCUSED ON WHY SOMETHING DIDN'T FLY.

24

25

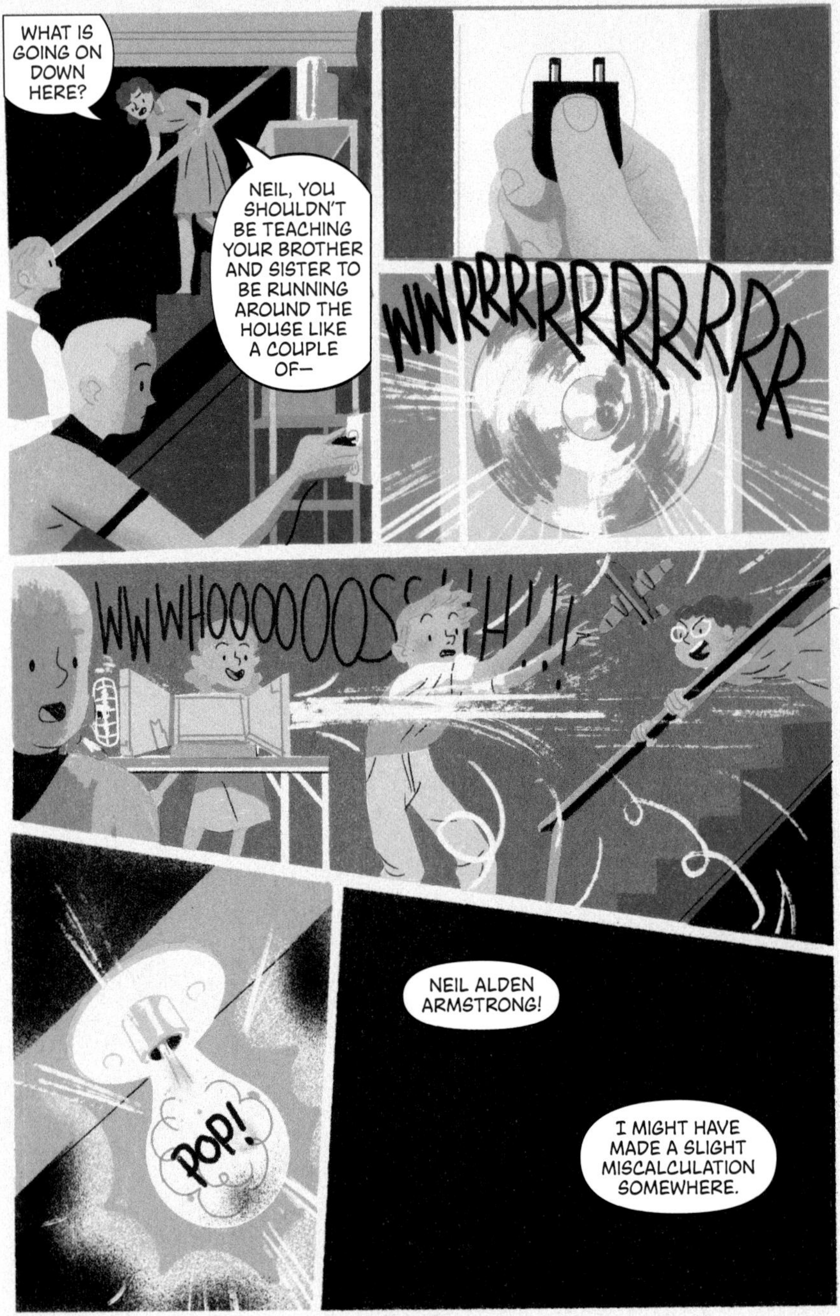
WHAT IS GOING ON DOWN HERE?
NEIL, YOU SHOULDN'T BE TEACHING YOUR BROTHER AND SISTER TO BE RUNNING AROUND THE HOUSE LIKE A COUPLE OF—
WWRRRRRRRRRRRR
WWWHOOOOOOOSSHH!!
POP!
NEIL ALDEN ARMSTRONG!
I MIGHT HAVE MADE A SLIGHT MISCALCULATION SOMEWHERE.

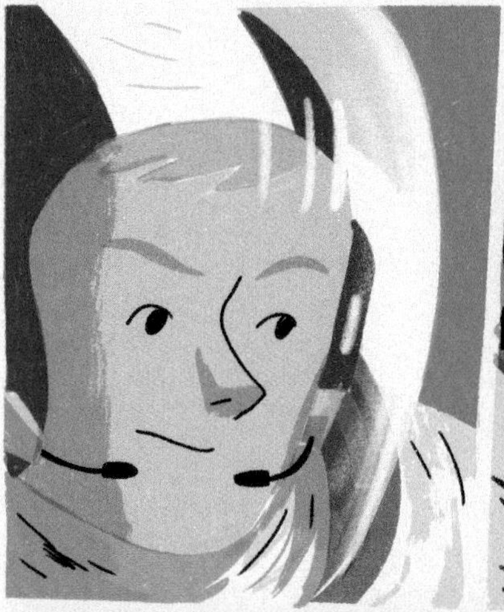

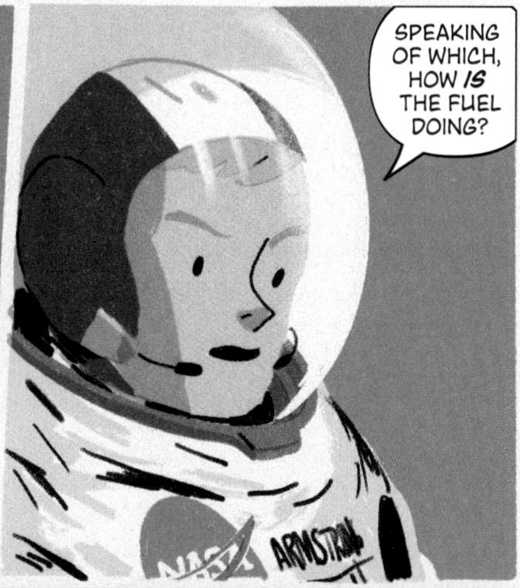
SPEAKING OF WHICH, HOW *IS* THE FUEL DOING?
NASA
ARMSTRONG

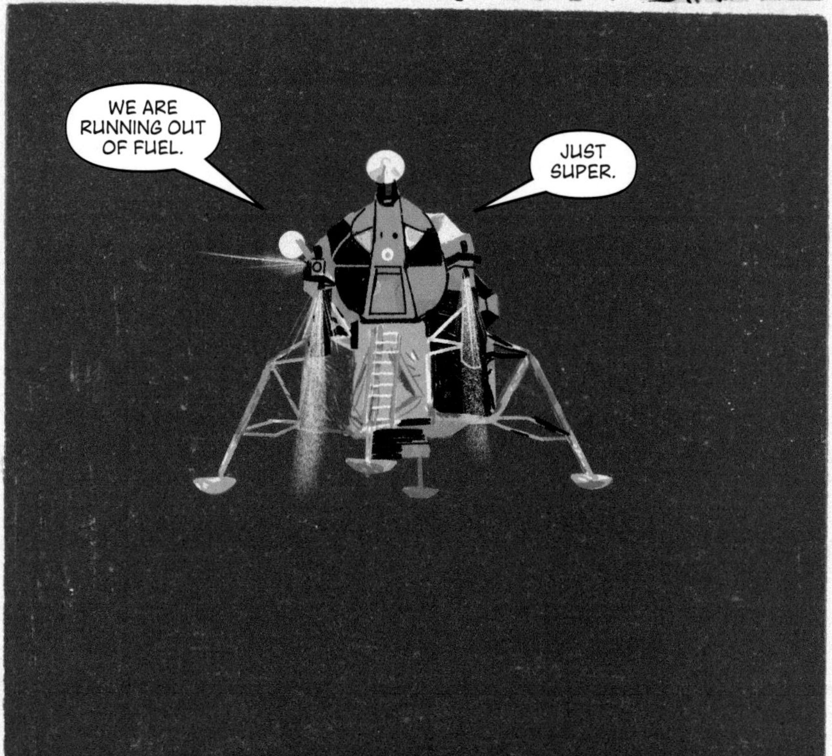
WE ARE RUNNING OUT OF FUEL.
JUST SUPER.

Buzz Aldrin

Buzz Aldrin (originally Edwin Eugene Aldrin Jr.) was born January 20, 1930, and grew up in Montclair, New Jersey. He earned the nickname Buzz because his sisters, Madeline and Fay Ann, would affectionately call him "brother," but with Fay Ann just learning how to speak, it sounded like she was saying "Buzzer."

After graduating third in his class at the United States Military Academy at West Point, Buzz became an Air Force pilot in the Korean War where he flew sixty-six highly dangerous missions. He then became a NASA pilot in 1963, in the third group of men selected to be astronauts. Three years later, he established a new record at the time for extravehicular activity (spacewalking!), spending a total of five and a half hours outside of the Gemini 12 spacecraft.

After the Apollo 11 mission, Buzz was awarded the Presidential Medal of Freedom in 1969 along with the rest of the crew members. Then, in 1972, after twenty-one years of service in the Air Force, he retired from active duty and in 2011 was awarded the Congressional Gold Medal.

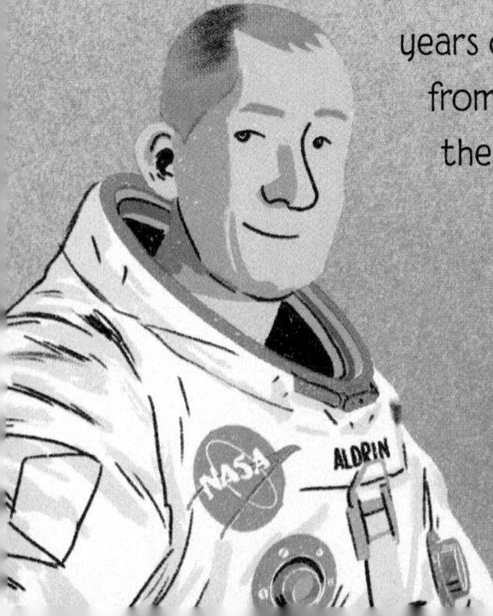
NASA
ALDRIN

WHEN NEIL WAS A TEENAGER, HE ENTERED THE BOWLING GREEN STATE UNIVERSITY SCIENCE FAIR.

HIS PROJECT WAS A STEAM TURBINE HE'D CRAFTED FROM SCRAPS OF WOOD AND A SMALL ALCOHOL LAMP.

IT RAN SO SMOOTHLY AND EFFICIENTLY THAT HE WAS SURE HE WOULD RECEIVE TOP MARKS.

BOWLING GREEN STATE UNIVERSITY
SCIENCE FAIR

34

35

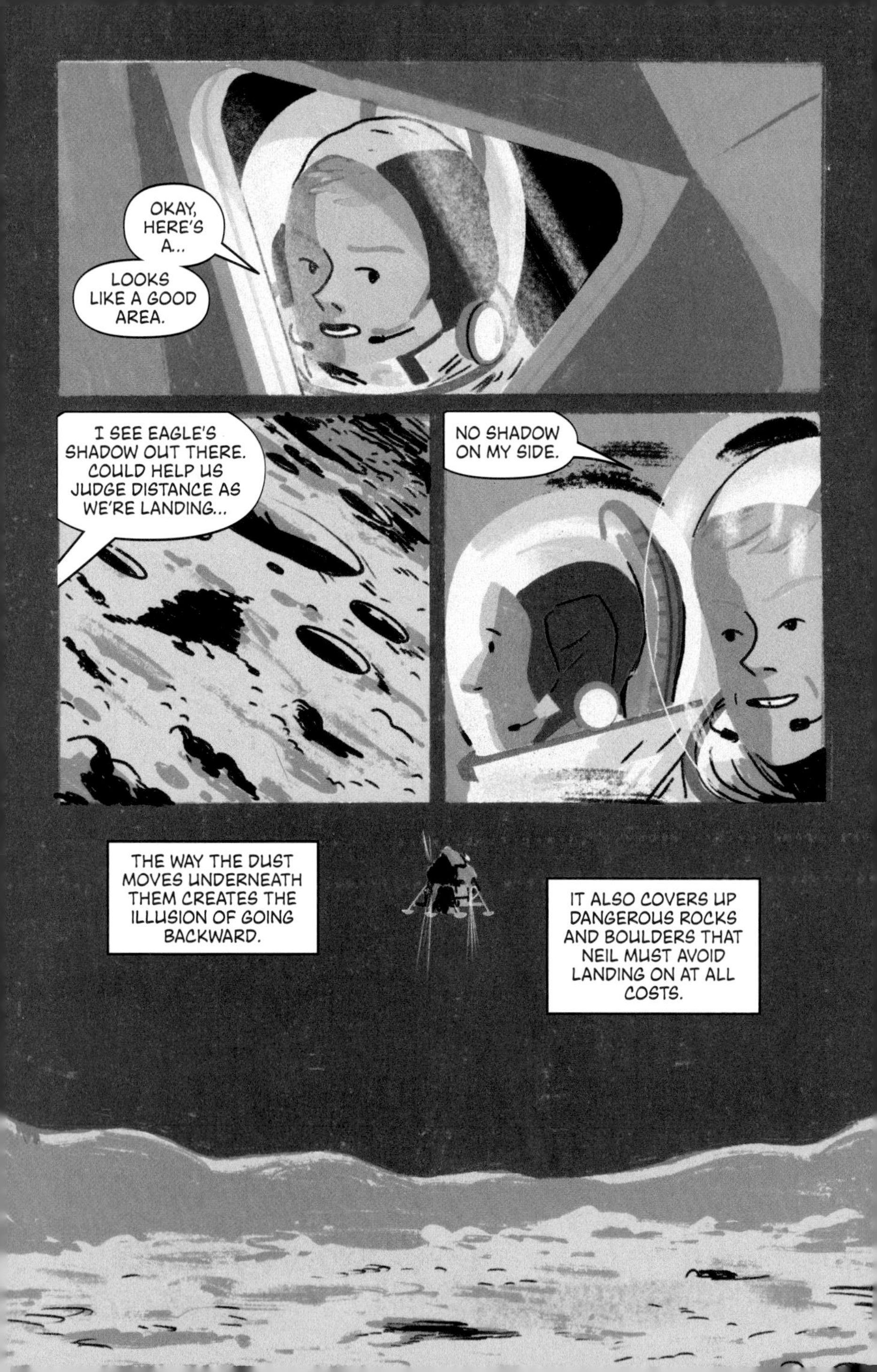

OKAY, HERE'S A...
LOOKS LIKE A GOOD AREA.
I SEE EAGLE'S SHADOW OUT THERE. COULD HELP US JUDGE DISTANCE AS WE'RE LANDING...
NO SHADOW ON MY SIDE.
THE WAY THE DUST MOVES UNDERNEATH THEM CREATES THE ILLUSION OF GOING BACKWARD.
IT ALSO COVERS UP DANGEROUS ROCKS AND BOULDERS THAT NEIL MUST AVOID LANDING ON AT ALL COSTS.

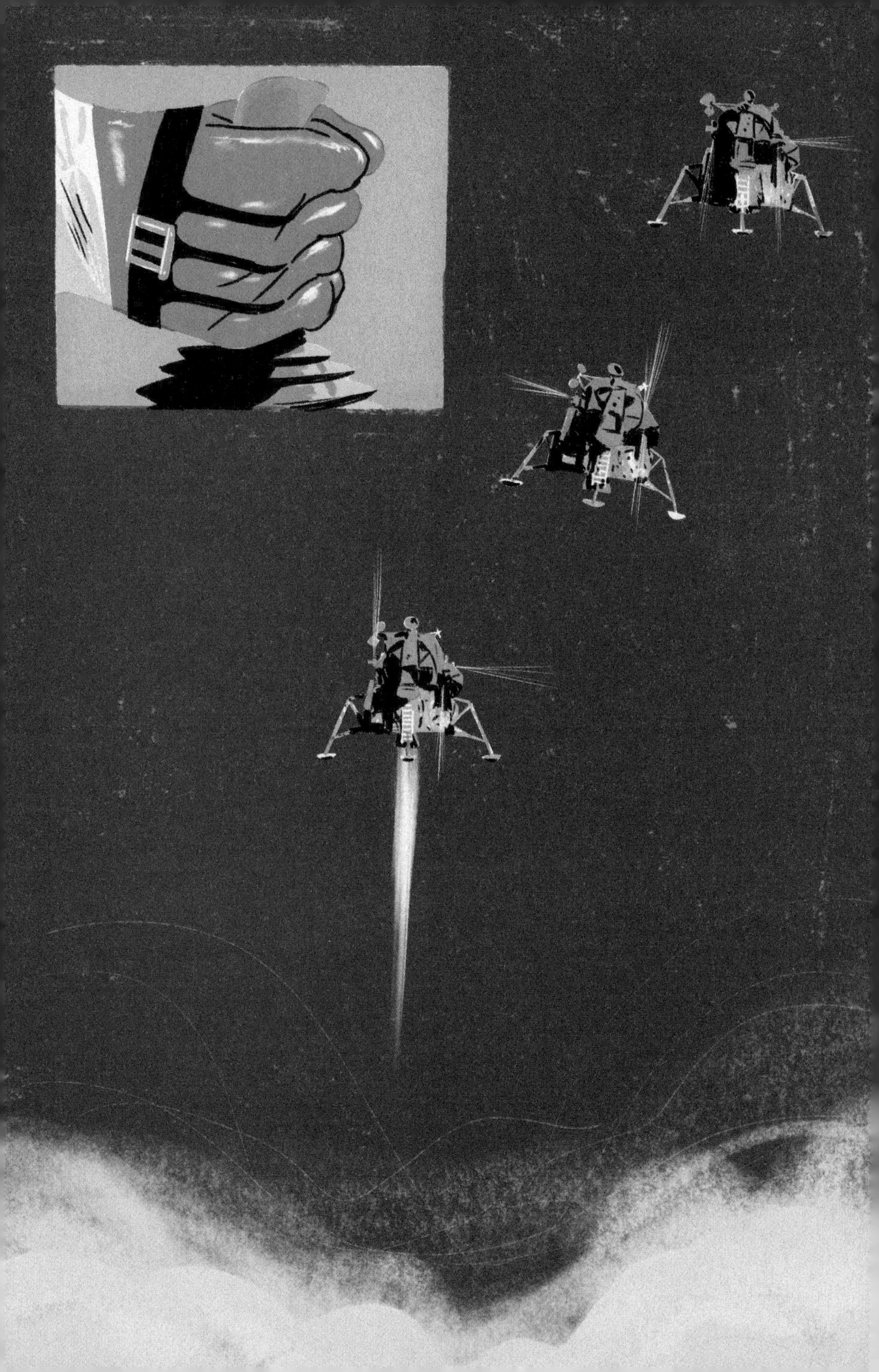

41

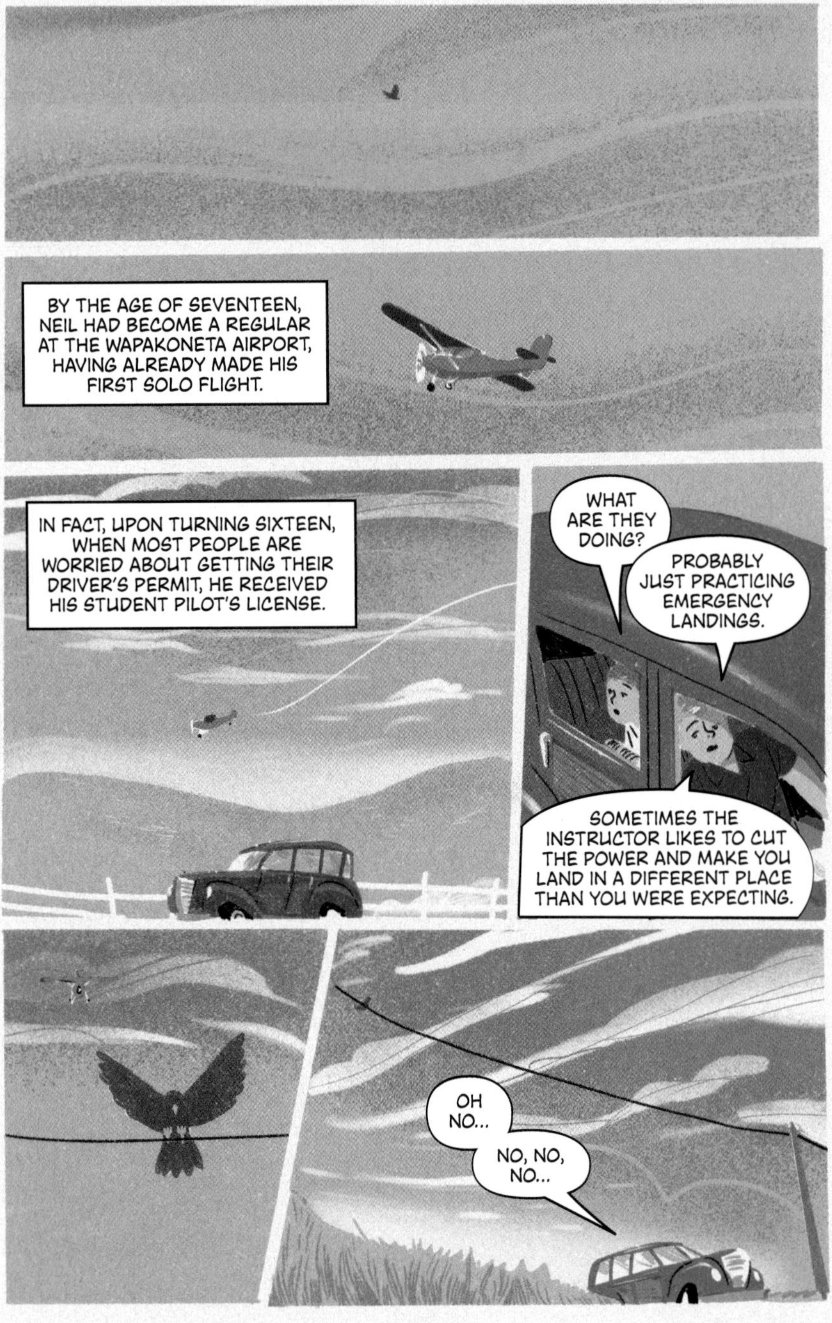
BY THE AGE OF SEVENTEEN, NEIL HAD BECOME A REGULAR AT THE WAPAKONETA AIRPORT, HAVING ALREADY MADE HIS FIRST SOLO FLIGHT.
IN FACT, UPON TURNING SIXTEEN, WHEN MOST PEOPLE ARE WORRIED ABOUT GETTING THEIR DRIVER'S PERMIT, HE RECEIVED HIS STUDENT PILOT'S LICENSE.
WHAT ARE THEY DOING?
PROBABLY JUST PRACTICING EMERGENCY LANDINGS.
SOMETIMES THE INSTRUCTOR LIKES TO CUT THE POWER AND MAKE YOU LAND IN A DIFFERENT PLACE THAN YOU WERE EXPECTING.
OH NO...
NO, NO, NO...

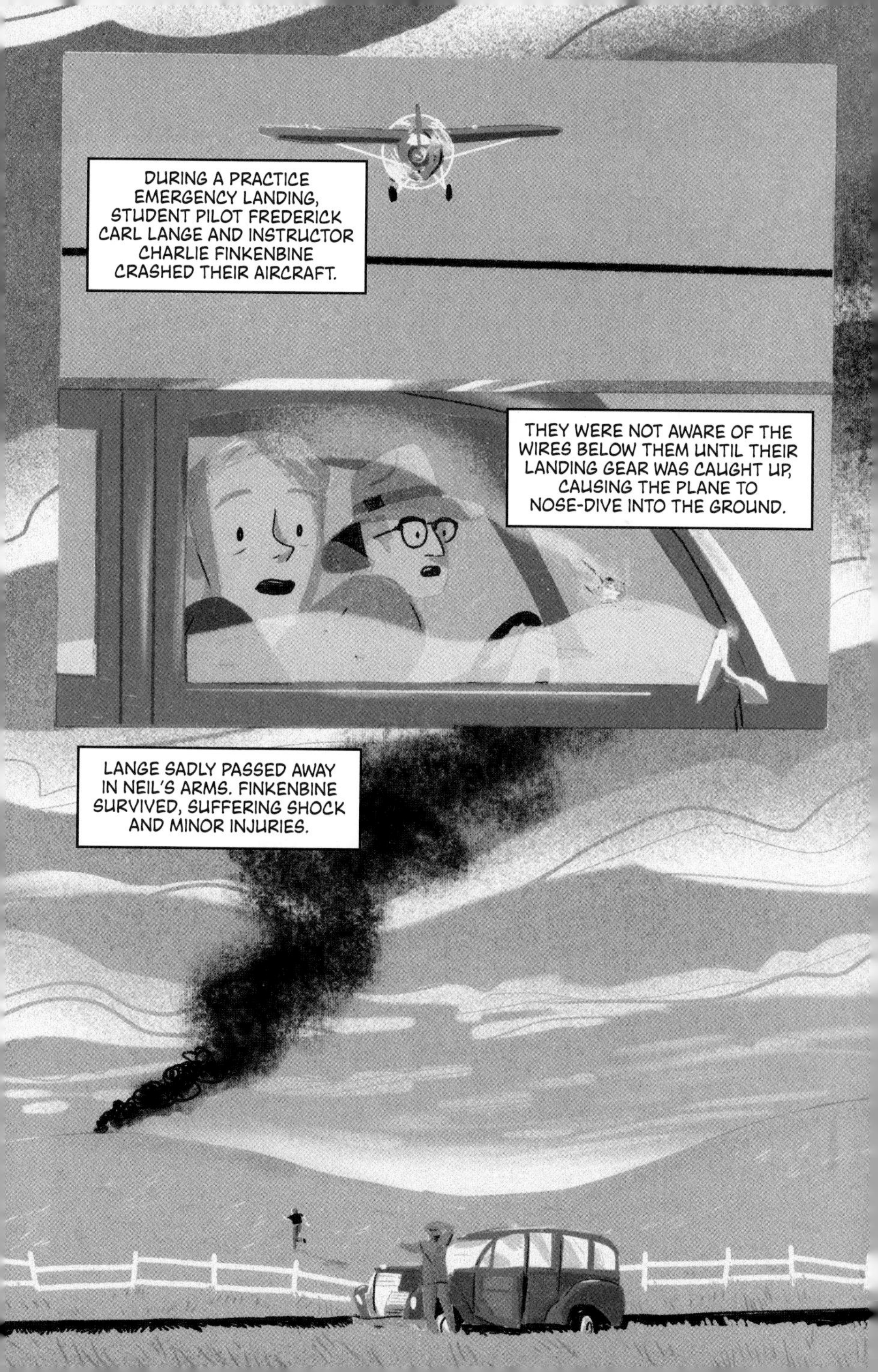
DURING A PRACTICE EMERGENCY LANDING, STUDENT PILOT FREDERICK CARL LANGE AND INSTRUCTOR CHARLIE FINKENBINE CRASHED THEIR AIRCRAFT.
THEY WERE NOT AWARE OF THE WIRES BELOW THEM UNTIL THEIR LANDING GEAR WAS CAUGHT UP, CAUSING THE PLANE TO NOSE-DIVE INTO THE GROUND.
LANGE SADLY PASSED AWAY IN NEIL'S ARMS. FINKENBINE SURVIVED, SUFFERING SHOCK AND MINOR INJURIES.

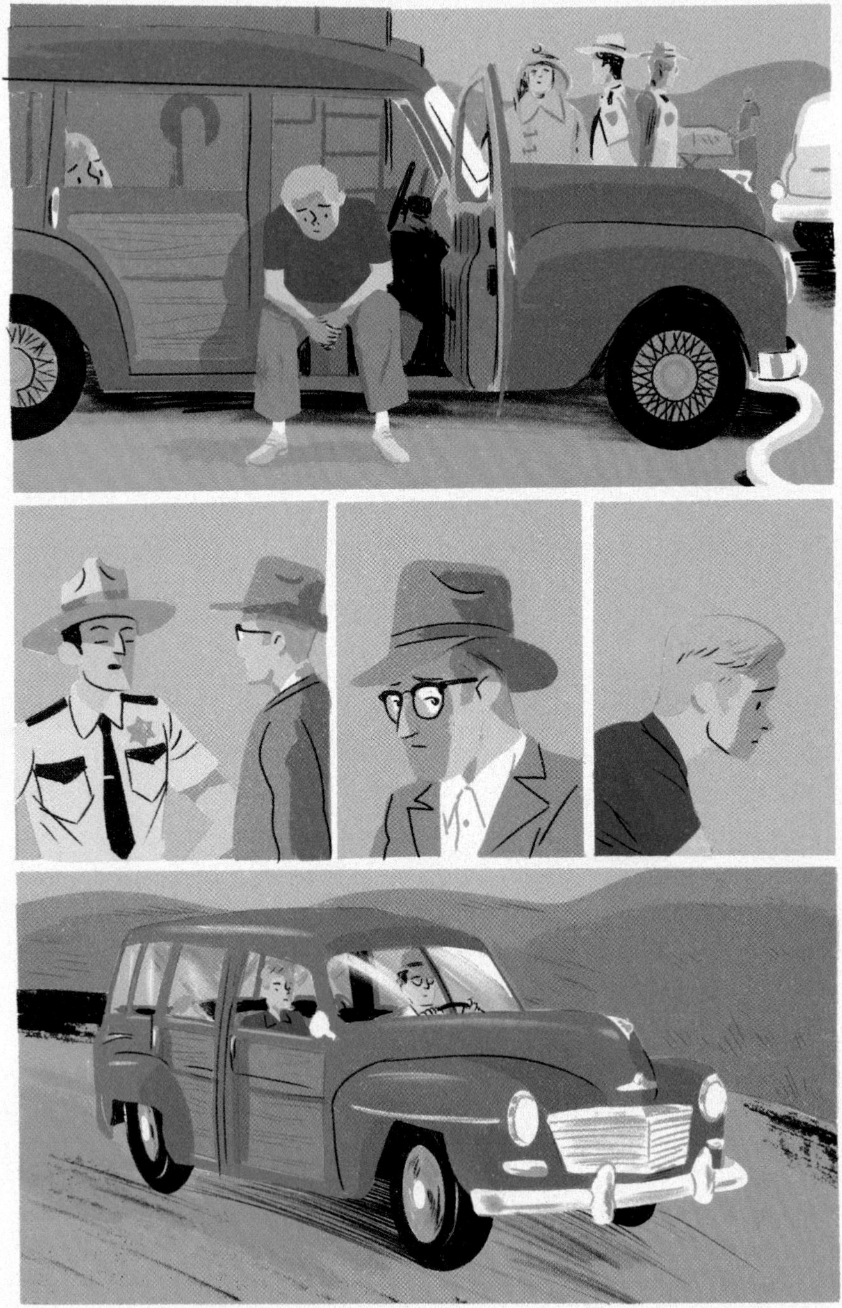

45

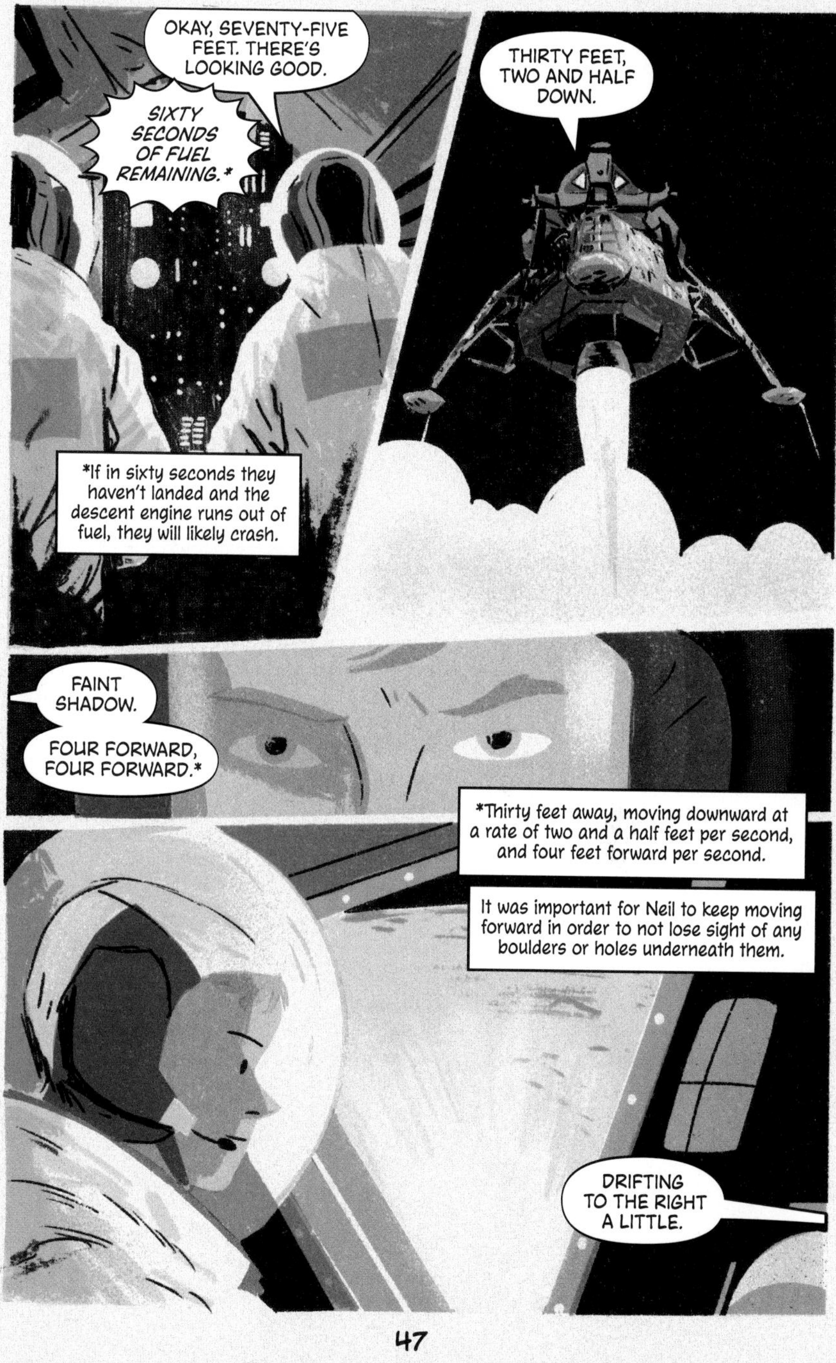
OKAY, SEVENTY-FIVE FEET. THERE'S LOOKING GOOD.
SIXTY SECONDS OF FUEL REMAINING.*
*If in sixty seconds they haven't landed and the descent engine runs out of fuel, they will likely crash.
THIRTY FEET, TWO AND HALF DOWN.
FAINT SHADOW.
FOUR FORWARD, FOUR FORWARD.*
*Thirty feet away, moving downward at a rate of two and a half feet per second, and four feet forward per second.
It was important for Neil to keep moving forward in order to not lose sight of any boulders or holes underneath them.
DRIFTING TO THE RIGHT A LITTLE.

48

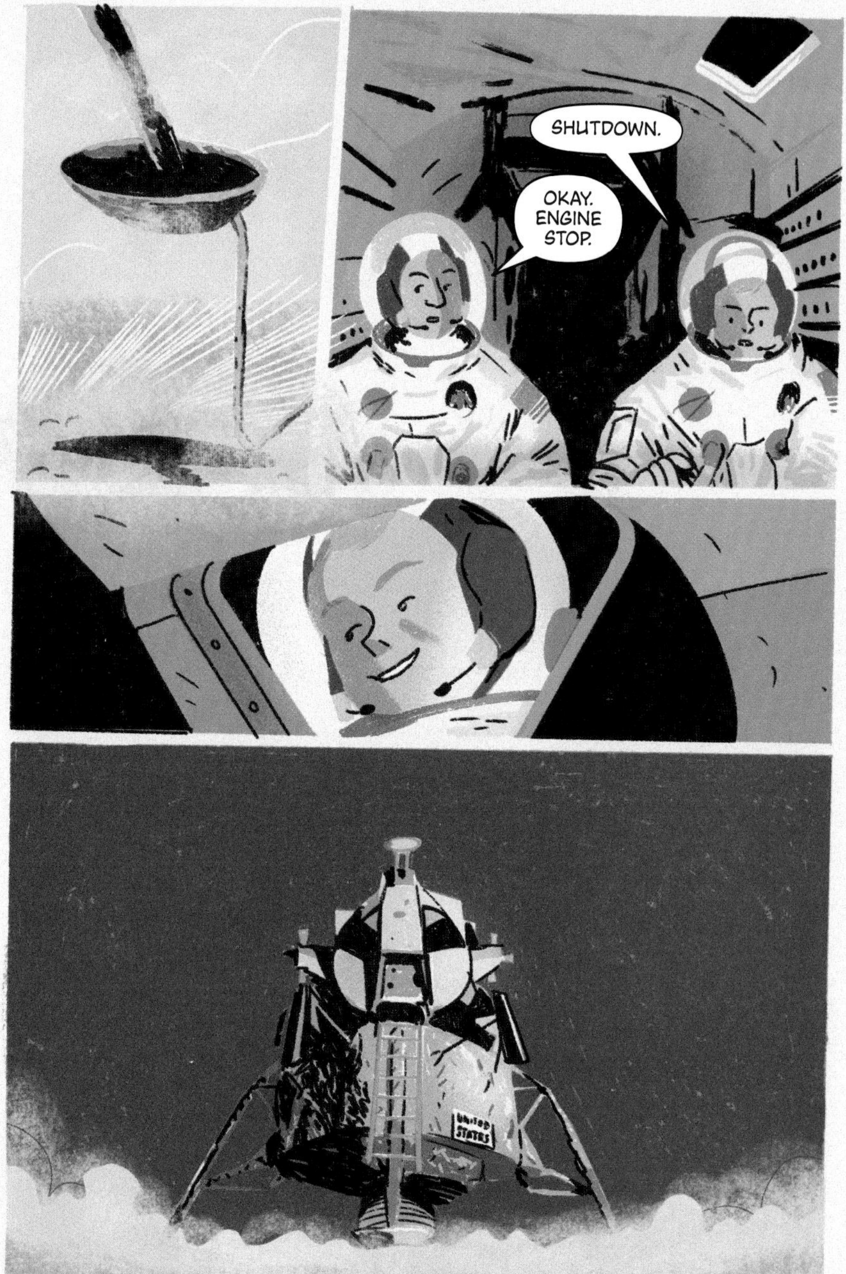
SHUTDOWN.
OKAY. ENGINE STOP.
United STATES

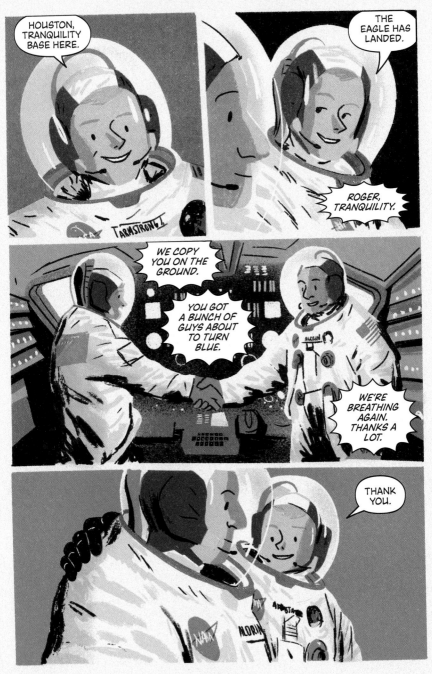

50

51

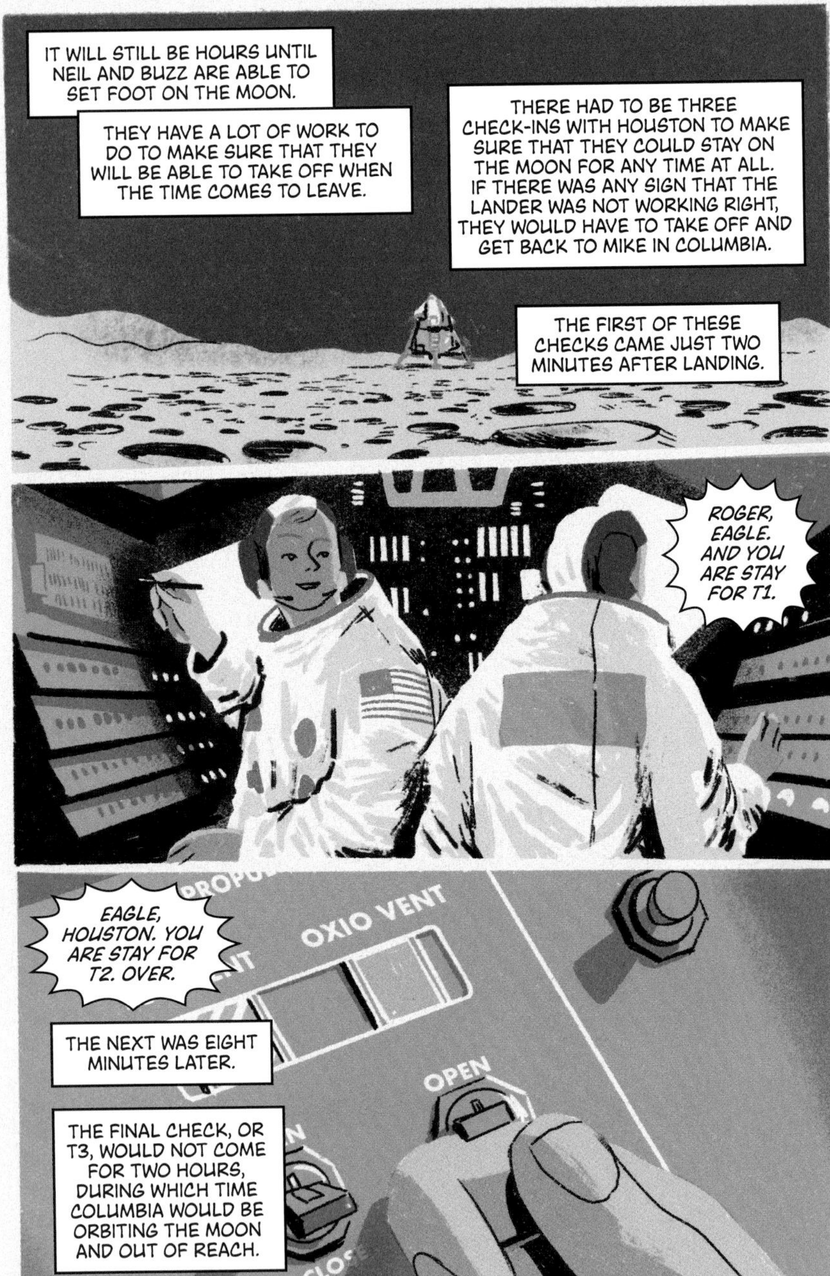
IT WILL STILL BE HOURS UNTIL NEIL AND BUZZ ARE ABLE TO SET FOOT ON THE MOON.
THEY HAVE A LOT OF WORK TO DO TO MAKE SURE THAT THEY WILL BE ABLE TO TAKE OFF WHEN THE TIME COMES TO LEAVE.
THERE HAD TO BE THREE CHECK-INS WITH HOUSTON TO MAKE SURE THAT THEY COULD STAY ON THE MOON FOR ANY TIME AT ALL. IF THERE WAS ANY SIGN THAT THE LANDER WAS NOT WORKING RIGHT, THEY WOULD HAVE TO TAKE OFF AND GET BACK TO MIKE IN COLUMBIA.
THE FIRST OF THESE CHECKS CAME JUST TWO MINUTES AFTER LANDING.
ROGER, EAGLE. AND YOU ARE STAY FOR T1.
EAGLE, HOUSTON. YOU ARE STAY FOR T2. OVER.
OXIO VENT
THE NEXT WAS EIGHT MINUTES LATER.
OPEN
THE FINAL CHECK, OR T3, WOULD NOT COME FOR TWO HOURS, DURING WHICH TIME COLUMBIA WOULD BE ORBITING THE MOON AND OUT OF REACH.

THE AREA OUT OF THE LEFT-HAND WINDOW IS A RELATIVELY LEVEL PLAIN, CRATERED WITH A FAIRLY LARGE NUMBER OF CRATERS OF THE FIVE TO FIFTY FOOT VARIETY, AND SOME RIDGES—SMALL, TWENTY, THIRTY FEET HIGH, I WOULD GUESS.
AND LITERALLY THOUSANDS OF LITTLE ONE- AND TWO-FOOT CRATERS AROUND THE AREA.
WE SEE SOME ANGULAR BLOCKS OUT SEVERAL HUNDRED FEET IN FRONT OF US THAT ARE PROBABLY TWO FEET IN SIZE AND HAVE ANGULAR EDGES.
THERE IS A HILL IN VIEW, JUST ABOUT ON THE GROUND TRACK AHEAD OF US. DIFFICULT TO ESTIMATE, BUT MIGHT BE HALF A MILE OR A MILE.

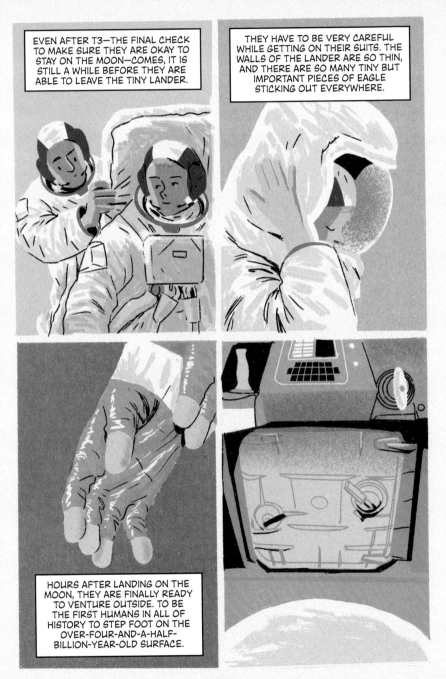

EVEN AFTER T3—THE FINAL CHECK TO MAKE SURE THEY ARE OKAY TO STAY ON THE MOON—COMES, IT IS STILL A WHILE BEFORE THEY ARE ABLE TO LEAVE THE TINY LANDER.

THEY HAVE TO BE VERY CAREFUL WHILE GETTING ON THEIR SUITS. THE WALLS OF THE LANDER ARE SO THIN, AND THERE ARE SO MANY TINY BUT IMPORTANT PIECES OF EAGLE STICKING OUT EVERYWHERE.

HOURS AFTER LANDING ON THE MOON, THEY ARE FINALLY READY TO VENTURE OUTSIDE. TO BE THE FIRST HUMANS IN ALL OF HISTORY TO STEP FOOT ON THE OVER-FOUR-AND-A-HALF-BILLION-YEAR-OLD SURFACE.

NASA Space Suit

One of the many things scientists at NASA had to figure out before going into space, let alone landing on the moon, was how the astronauts could survive without any air. This is why in every picture of an astronaut on a mission, they are wearing those oversize suits.

These are called pressure suits, or extravehicular mobility units (EMUs), and they provide the external pressure the astronauts need in order to make their lungs draw in breath when they are outside of the spacecraft.

Before getting into the suits, however, the astronauts had to put on a cooling unit, which circulates cool water in order to keep body temperatures down when wearing the airtight suits. Other elements of the suit included thick boots that were able to withstand temperatures from 250 degrees above zero to 250 degrees below; gloves covered with a fine metal mesh to prevent the more vulnerable layers from cuts and tears; a "Snoopy cap" which was a soft hood that had earphones and a microphone; and a helmet shaped like a big goldfish bowl, with a two-layered shield coated in gold to protect the astronauts from the dangerous rays of the sun.

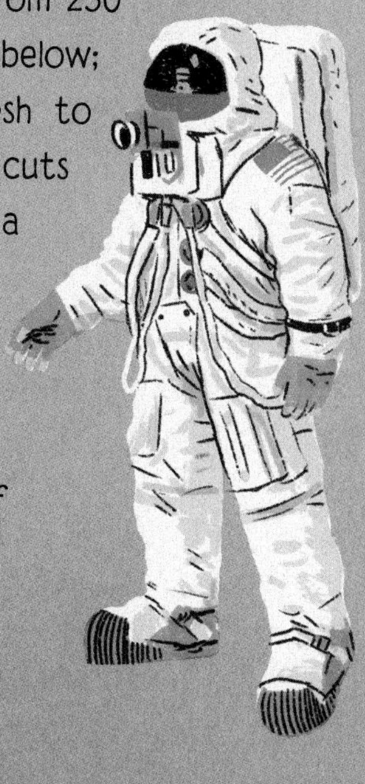

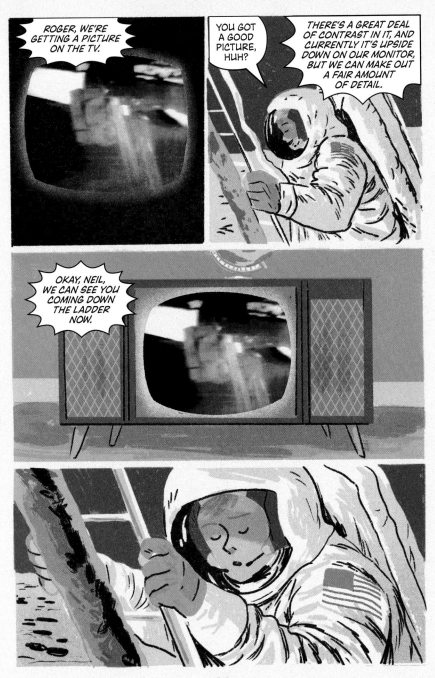

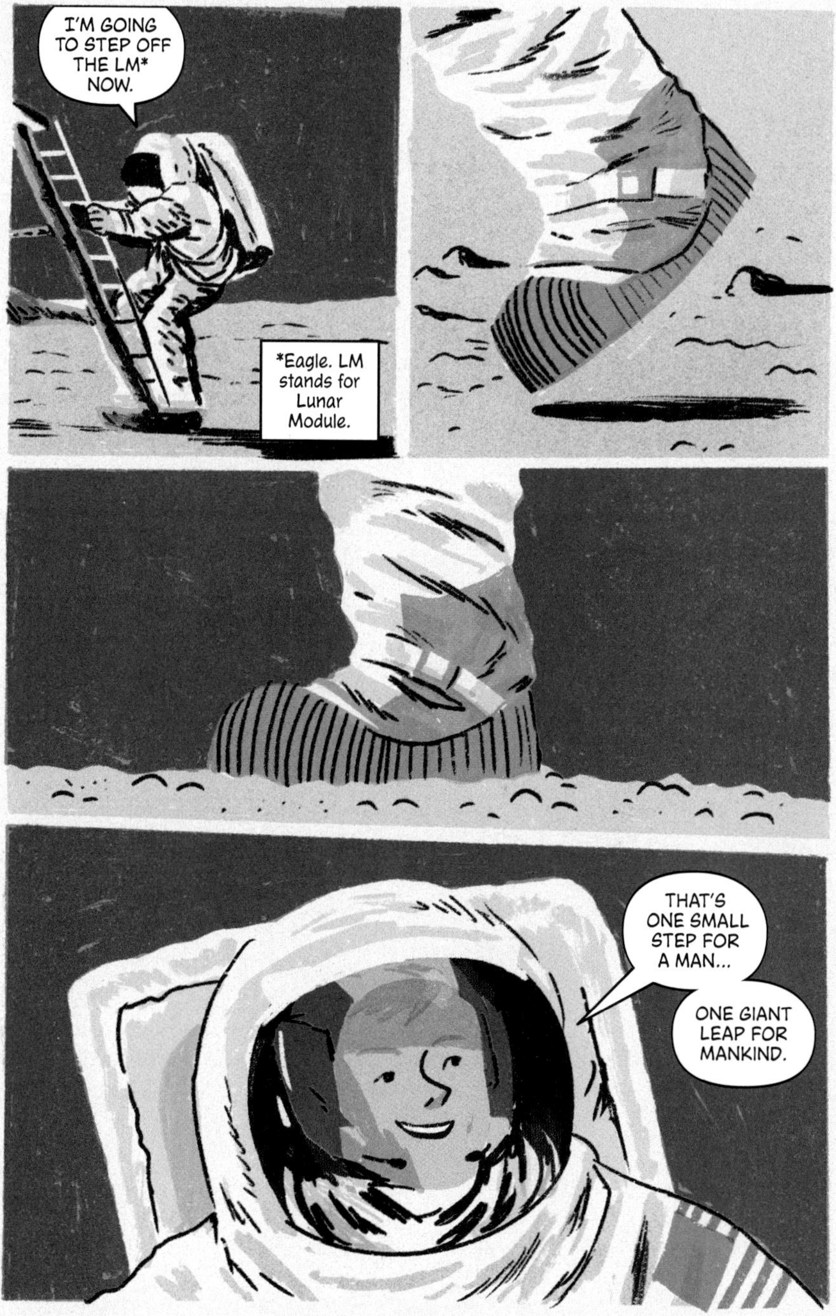
I'M GOING TO STEP OFF THE LM* NOW.
*Eagle. LM stands for Lunar Module.
THAT'S ONE SMALL STEP FOR A MAN...
ONE GIANT LEAP FOR MANKIND.

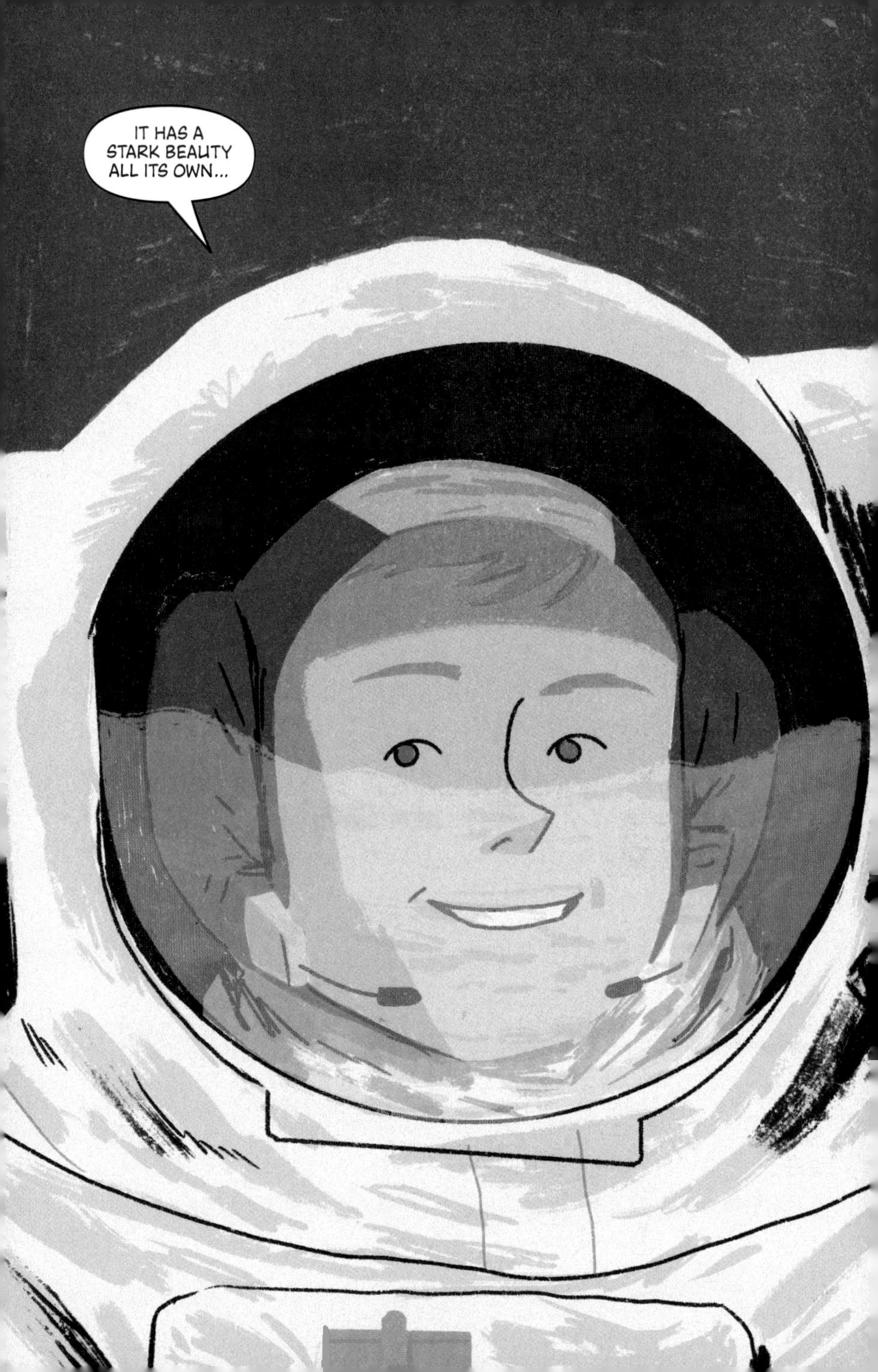
IT HAS A STARK BEAUTY ALL ITS OWN...

Conclusion

Neil Armstrong's journey to the moon began long before Apollo 11, Gemini 8, or even being named an astronaut. It started in a small Ohio town in the 1930s, where, as a young boy, Neil's dream of a life of flying became a reality, and he learned the lessons that would mold him into the person we celebrate today. The first man to walk on the moon.

Like Mike and Buzz, Neil was also the recipient of the Presidential Medal of Freedom in 1969 and the Congressional Gold Medal in 2011, as well as many other awards and honors. After retiring from NASA, Neil was a professor at the University of Cincinnati from 1971 to 1979, teaching engineering courses in aircraft design and experimental flight.

In 2011, at the age of eighty-one, Neil was greatly troubled with where the future of human space exploration was headed, especially in the United States. In a rare public appearance, he gave a speech to the Committee on Science, Space, and Technology of the House of Representatives, where he pointed to a lack of money and direction in the program, as well as a need for more imagination and creativity, as his areas of main concern.

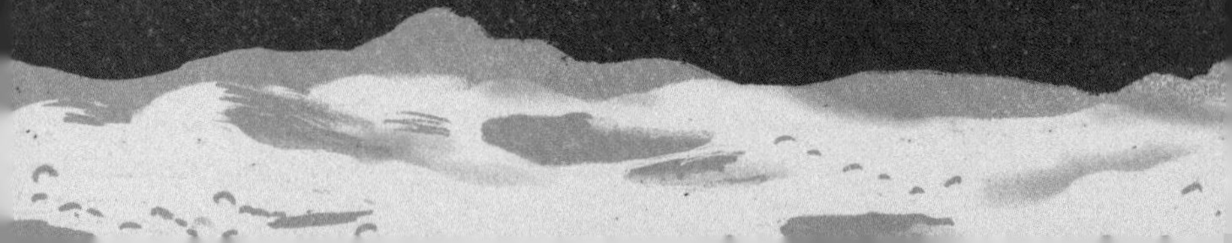

Neil died on August 25, 2012, at the age of eighty-two. He used his last public appearances and interviews to speak about the work the United States and NASA had to do over the coming years to get back to the lunar surface. Yet, even with his concerns, he was confident that someday, before too long, people would again walk on the moon.

"I know one day, somebody is going to go fly back up there and pick up that camera I left," he said.

That, of course, begs the question . . .

Anyone feel up for a trip?

Just 480,000 miles to the moon and back again.

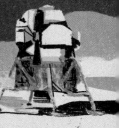

Timeline of Neil Armstrong's Life

1930 — Neil Armstrong is born on August 5 in Wapakoneta, Ohio

1932 — Neil Armstrong's father takes him to his first air show
and his parents give him his first model plane

1937 — Goes on his first airplane flight

1938 — Attempts, and fails, to climb the tree in his backyard

1946 — Earns his pilot's license

1947 — Graduates high school; witnesses the plane crash;
begins attending Purdue University

1949 — Reports for military duty

1955 — Graduates from Purdue

1956 — Marries Janet Shearon

1962 — Neil is selected for the second group of NASA
astronauts

1966 — Commands Gemini 8 mission

1969 — Completes Apollo 11 mission; receives Presidential
Medal of Freedom

1971 — Leaves NASA to teach at the University of Cincinnati

1994 — Neil and Janet are divorced

— Marries Carol Held Knight

2011 — Receives Congressional Gold Medal

2012 — Dies on August 25 at eighty-two years old

Bibliography

*Books for young readers

"Apollo 11: Technical Air-to-Ground Voice Transcription." Apollo Lunar Surface Journal. https://history.nasa.gov/alsj/a11/a11transcript_tec.html.

Armstrong, Neil, Edwin Aldrin, and Michael Collins. "Man walks on another world." *National Geographic*, December 1969, 738–749.

Barbree, Jay. *Neil Armstrong: A Life of Flight*. New York: Thomas Dunne Books, 2014.

*Edwards, Roberta. *Who Was Neil Armstrong?* New York: Penguin Workshop, 2008.

Engle, Michael. *Landing Eagle: Inside the Cockpit During the First Moon Landing*. Dublin, Ohio: Telemachus Press, 2019.

Fairhead, D., dir. *Armstrong*. 2019. United States/UK: Tin Goose Films, Haviland Digital, Mark Stewart Productions, Hays Films.

Hansen, James R. *First Man: The Life of Neil A. Armstrong*. New York: Simon & Schuster, 2005.

*Howard, Martin. *The Extraordinary Life of Neil Armstrong*. London: Puffin Books, 2019.

Parry, Dan. *Moonshot: The Inside Story of Mankind's Greatest Adventure*. London: Ebury Press, 2009.

*Weakland, Mark. *When Neil Armstrong Built a Wind Tunnel*. North Mankato, MN: Picture Window Books, 2018.

Weaver, Kenneth. "The flight of Apollo 11: 'One giant leap for mankind.'" *National Geographic*, December 1969, 752–787.

ABOUT THE CREATORS

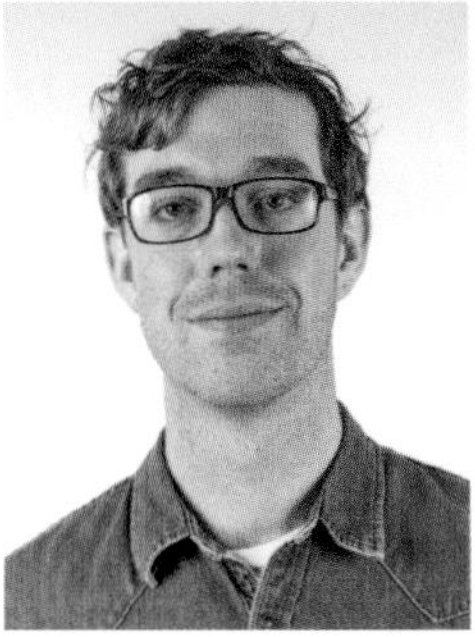

Nathan Page was born in Kingston, Ontario, where he began writing at an early age. He now lives in Toronto with his cat, Marlowe. He is the writer of the graphic novel *The Montague Twins: The Witch's Hand.*

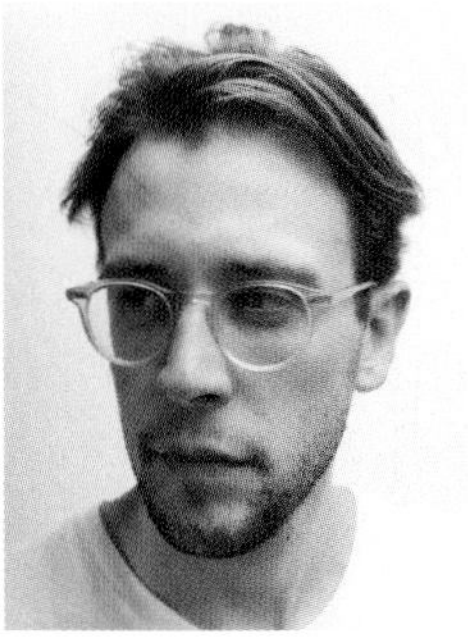

MIKE PEREIRA

Drew Shannon (he/him) is a Toronto-based illustrator whose debut graphic novel, *The Montague Twins: The Witch's Hand*, was published by Random House Graphics in July 2020.